AF508694

Every Now and Again:
The Poems of a Lifetime

Edmund J. McDevitt

Every Now and Again: The Poems of a Lifetime by Edmund J. McDevitt

Cover and interior designed by Ellie Searl, Publishista®

Print Book ISBN: 9798988353904
Ebook ISBN: 9798988353911
LCCN: 2023911370

Deep Time Publishing
Oak Park, IL

Contents

Dedication 7

Preface 9

Recent Poems - 2017-2022 11

   Charles III 13

   Flight 15

   Copernica 18

   Look Up! 21

   Ostinato in E 24

   Every now and again 26

   Polar Vortex Song 27

   Spring Arrived 28

   Autumn Has Intruded 31

   Let's Do This A Different Way 35

   Blackbirds 38

   Rain Refraction 41

   Impressionist Encounter 42

   A Season Postponed 44

   Upon Passing the Baton 46

   Perepeteia 49

   What I Might Have Done 50

Contents

Earlier Poems 53

Adelaide Crapsey (1878 – 1914) 55

Cinquains 56

Other Cinquains 57

Plain Sense 59

Sunday 61

Off the Main Line 63

The Cape Highway 65

Relations 66

Vesper Silhouette 67

Shaman of Spring 68

At the Clinic 71

Life 73

Continued 75

Chairs 77

Flight 83 79

Dream in G 80

Eubie 82

About the Author 85

Dedication

I dedicate this little volume to all who did not know I wrote poetry, because I didn't tell you; and to all who did know and were over-kind; and to those of you who will never know you were the inspiration for one or another poem in this book. To those I have loved and who have loved me back, I especially give this book to you, whether you're here to see it or not. And to those who prodded me to love language and to wish to use it well and truly, I give you these words as small proof that you either succeeded or failed.

Preface

I've written poems since, well, a long time ago. The poems in this book fall into two general time bands: the early 1970s to the 1980s; the period from 2019 to the present.

Why the hiatus? Can't explain it, other than to say that my mind was too busy to do the thinking poetry requires; to observe, to record the observations; to heed a stop sign and just sit.

I looked for critics but, as is so often the case, the ones I tapped felt compelled to extol the wonderfulness they thought I sought. Only rarely did someone ask, "Well, what is this about? Why should I be reading it?" Perfectly fine questions, but, as I say, rare. Even back in the early stages.

So I let them – the poems, not the critics - sit and age, perhaps molder. Often a poem will just need quiet time without my intrusion. Then, when I knock and enter it again, it is different, sometimes needing a paint job or new plumbing, or just plumbing at all.

Tinkering is a nasty habit. It makes every sort of sense to stop placing commas, seeking a nicer word, looking to use the foot pump of meaning. A poem lives or it doesn't, and how I perceive its life is necessarily going to be different from how a reader does, of course. Really, if I'm tinkering, I'm changing things for myself, since nobody is asking for the tinker to tinker.

It's time to let these go, to give them whatever start in life they can have. I have other things to do.

- Edmund J. McDevitt

RECENT POEMS - 2017-2022

CHARLES III

Written while watching *King Charles III* on PBS and in response to a friend who emailed me during the program, saying, ""But soft, I cannot stay awake." The movie is written in blank verse.

Awake you would have seen the tragic end
    When lit, that fire of puissance brings
    about;
A gracious, aging king late to the throne,
Lets blind intransigence bring down his reign,
A downfall made the more a certainty
By plotting queen to be, the crafty Kate.
'Tis sad, no, more than sad, the sorry end
That faces Charles, whose throne is not yet
    warm.
His triumph, stolen from him by his son.,
His very life dissolvéd, ee'n as he
Dissolves the Parliament and sends them
    home.

And irony abounds: his precedent
Comes from the king whose name his
　　treach'rous son
Will wear as he accepts his usurped
　　crown.

2017

Flight

FROM green to gray we traveled,
From a world full of Spring singing
To a world awaiting song.
The ice below was water just a bit ago,
The sea behind us now the frozen lake ahead.
A few blinks of one's eye
And the cypress turn to towers of glass,
The dense mangroves to dots of brown-leaved
bur oak.
Our escape has failed again,
But still we've been beguiled by a tapestry of
color,
Heard a raucous choir
That will ripple toward us in its time,
Follow us without our bidding,
Without our intervention.

We went hoping to urge it along
Or, perhaps, to remind ourselves that it will
arrive

While getting some chill out of our bones.
We returned. The chill returned.
We, grudging, took it with us each week as we
    searched,
We drove around our winter garden, peering
    here, hoping there.
We lamented the skunk cabbage.
It seemed to be in refusal.
But then miraculously it appeared, overnight,
Green and red in its swampy hollow.

It was, in its own way, an understatement.
A quiet admonition:
Stop. Be still.
Soon enough, soon enough the song will begin.
What still lies waiting underground will find
    the sun.
Impatient hope arises from the cold
The endless wind
The steel skies
The wan sun in the south
The stifling cocoon of clothing.

Perhaps one year, after all these years,
We'll let it happen on its own.

We'll not natter
That this one is worse
This one is the beast of beasts.
Perhaps.

Or we'll fly again to where Spring is
Hoping to drag it back with us.
Hoping that this time it will work.

April 2019

COPERNICA

DID I hear you correctly?
Did you say
    That the nova that recently appeared
The star that exploded
Is in our "near neighborhood?"
The one that it is a million light years away?
Am I to understand that
The explosion that we just saw
Happened a million years ago
And we're just now getting the news?
I guess I understand.
That distance is 1/13,000 of the way to the edge
    of our universe
Hardly noticeable, really -

But to my mind, it's roughly the same
As the distance between me and Copernicus.

I'd love to visit Copernicus, actually.
But I can no more get back to his time,
I can no more see his life
Than I can hope to get over next door in the near
    neighborhood
To see that exploding sun.

Oh, of course, you're right:
I can visit Copernicus in his writings.
But don't you think that's thin gruel for a visit?
However bright the light his ideas cast,
I can only try to imagine
What he talked about one day to the next,
All that he didn't write down.

We saw that dying star suddenly.
We watch it on our own schedule, don't we?
As if it were collapsing right now, day by day.
But it's been a million years plus the time we've
    been watching it,
The lifetime of humans on Earth
Since it obliterated all around it.
The heat and bright light of that sun
Are no nearer to me
Than are the voice and odors of Copernicus.
But still, I wonder,
Did a Copernica and her writings perish
In the near neighborhood of that sun?
Did everything a whole world accomplished
Become mere atoms in a moment,
Not a one of them bearing witness to her
    brilliance?

I suppose I could mourn Copernica
And all of the Copernicas lost out there
In one near neighborhood or another,
But if you don't mind,
I'll look for one in my here and now
Who could be a sudden bright light.
Do you know of one such as that?
In the neighborhood? Nearby?

Let me know.
I'll be in the neighborhood.

April 2020

Look Up!

I tell you!
I tell you, Look Up!
   Look there. And there.
You've walked this path

Again and again.
But what have you seen?

I ask you!
I ask you, What is between
Where you started
And where you are going?

That world inside you,
The place you go to

As you walk this path

Day in, day out -
It's a fine world, as worlds go
But how different is it
From yesterday to today?

That destination you're trudging to
With such narrowed vision

Day in, day out –
How would it be
Were the path strewn with the joy, the shock
Of the undiscovered
The things that have been there to see?
Tell me!
Tell me what you see!
Is it a tree? A bridge? A bird diving into the
    water?
Is it a parade?
Does that fountain always erupt that way?

Look around!
Look around at those near you
Eyes down, staring at screens.
Turn your gaze up. Just up. That's all.
Some of them, perhaps enough of them,
Will glance up too, wondering:
What are you looking at?

And soon you'll have a community,
A congeries,
A true movement
Of lookers, of seekers, of discoverers,
Myriad interior landscapes abandoned
Just because one day
You looked up. And over there. And there.

Don't stop!
Don't ever stop,
Now that you're a silent prophet of looking.

The quotidian procession is always new, always
    fresh,
Always ripe for an awakening or two,
And you and those you've made to raise their
    eyes
Have become a pandemic of looking,
You multipliers of discovery.

One day, tell me,
Tell me what you've found!
And I'll tell you, if you want to know.
Perhaps we've seen the same thing,
Though differently.
But we've seen.

November 2019

OSTINATO IN E

THE wonder of it
Is that after all that time,
After almost a human generation burrowing in
    darkness,
Making not a sound –
They struggle upward through the softened
    earth,
Climb a tree and transform to fly about,
And begin their unrehearsed song
In a pitch, that if perfect enough
Will gain them a moment of ecstasy
And a quick demise,
Starting the cycle over again.

They don't think much,
As far as I know.
They don't hold seminars underground
As far as I know.
As far as anyone knows,
They don't write or agonize
About the meaning of it all.

For them it's all in that song and that ecstatic
    moment.
Of no particular moment.
For them the journey's end is enough.
It is.
They do.
It is enough.
    June 2007

EVERY NOW AND AGAIN

EVERY now and again
I have moments of clarity
Moments of bright light
In the passing blur,
Sometimes dead stops of aha!
Other times sudden suspicion
That I've had it wrong.

It's only every now and again
That crystals of understanding
Rise into the light and remain
So that I can say,
Every now and again,
That I know now
What I didn't know for sure
And that chances are good
That it can happen
Again.

January 2019

Polar Vortex Song

(sung to an obvious tune)

CHESTNUTS freezing in an open field
Jack Frost nipping off your nose
    Warm-weather songs being cried by a choir
And folks dressed up like Eskimos.
Everybody knows big mittens and some
    Toastytoes
Help to warm your hands and feet.
Shivering folks with their boots full of snow
Are hugging strangers just for heat.
We know that Spring is on its way
But months from now, so there's no hope for it
    today.
Now every mother's child is gonna say
That clothing layers make it really hard to play.
And so I'm offering this simple phrase
To kids from one to ninety-two
Although it's been said many times, many
    ways
Polar vortex to yoooooooooouuuuuuu.

March 2020

SPRING ARRIVED

SUDDENLY, overnight, the trees are budding.
A cardinal is claiming territory.
Here in our plague year, we have not
noticed.
We look inward
We look at each other.
And Spring is here, ready or not.

We humans have been brought to ground
By an unseeable, unfathomable thing
That doesn't think
Doesn't even live, as we know life;
It leads a "borrowed life,"
Just chemicals until it finds us.

While we hide
While we hold each other apart
While we watch this otherwise inert ball of spines
Cut a swath across the landscape of our lives and
souls,
A tornado without scale.
We're missing Spring.
Migrating birds have arrived

Flying into newly clean air,
Plying in now-clear water
That we cannot foul as we hide.

Daffodils bloom riotously.
Other bulbs reach down
To get the foothold they need to push above
ground
But we're not present to see the yellow and the
blue,

Perhaps that mindless sphere, in its exuberance
at finding us,
Is having its own Spring, not meaning to bring
harm,
But just to multiply in celebration, to migrate
with the birds,
To travel with us as long as it can
Until it is cast back the into the non-being
From whence it came.

Meanwhile, we can release our fear,
Look outside,
Notice Spring in all its flower and movement.
It will happen with or without us.
It always does.
If we choose to be in it,

If we choose to savor it
Spring will welcome us -
Not with shouts and celebrations
But with quiet loud beauty.

Suddenly, overnight, the trees are budding.
A cardinal is announcing itself and its territory.
It's Spring.
    March 2020

Autumn Has Intruded

AUTUMN has intruded itself on our
summer.
     So many birds that had planned to
  migrate
Have already flown by;
The thrushes, the late warblers,
The kinglets and sparrows who'd been up
     north
Were foraging fiercely and have left.
A Brown Creeper hit a building in the city
And waited on the pavement to recover.
Siskins are here now with still-raucous Jays
And the sparrows that nested in the Arctic.
The jarring cold will drive them south soon.

Yellowing leaves fall outside our window.
Tomato plants become compost.
The flowers on our balcony.
Lush and prolific just a moment ago,
Have shot their stems, gone to seed.
We've uprooted some of the survivors,
And a hopeful nasturtium

Has sprouted in the soil of one of the denuded
    pots.
Frost will soon take that and the ones we don't
    bring in
And they'll blow ceaselessly in the winter
    wind.

We, meanwhile, remain masked and muted
Against the random raging of
A bit of code that seems, in all its blind
    innocence,
To have an imperative: Be fruitful and
    multiply.
It does not have worry genes or a conscience
Or respect for personal space.
Its sense of limits, if it has one, is not that of its
    brothers and sisters,
The ones that only make us sneeze and cough
    and wheeze.
It goes everywhere in a body,
Leaving detritus in its path of destruction,
A trail of fogged thought, debilitation, and
    death for some

A lasting memory of days and weeks lost for
    others,
And a helplessness it neither intends nor
    knows.
Nor does it know of its urge to be more of
    itself.
It simply is.

In our plague year
We dodge and weave, warding off this blind
    protobeing,
To get on with our lives
indoors apart from almost all we know.
We go out with care,
Our only defense outside,
Unless we pull along a sanitizer cart
Or a portable ultraviolet generator.

No matter.
The little beast rages. It knows nothing.
Nothing of those who mask against it,
Nothing of those who claim their rights
    against it
It simply is, while we abide our fear.

Outside it will soon be leafless, lacking color
But we persist. We burn logs against the lost
    sun.
We festoon our corners, our cabinets, our
    lamps
With greenery and flowers. We tell our
    families
To stay away.

Suddenly, overnight, the season is brown
A cardinal searches for food
It's winter.

October　2020

LET'S LOOK AT THIS A DIFFERENT WAY

LET'S look at this a different way.
Let's look at it as if
Snow has fallen
Obscuring everything we think we know
Our landmarks gone
Our touchstones invisible.
Look at this without our map
The bends and twists
The intersections
The paths laid out by long-ago minds
Who tell us still the how and the where
The stops and starts
The speed, direction, the way to move.
If we look with fear
Where the sound we're hearing comes from
Across the snow
Where no path is yet laid,
Where the pits and roots are hidden,
Where unknown malevolence might lurk
We might decide that the old path is best
That the risk is too great
That the assurance of our insurance isn't
    enough.

We ought to look at insurance, by the way,
For what it guarantees, for how it makes us
    safe.
It protects us, we think.
But only after something has occurred.
It is not a shield against danger;
It pays after the damage is done,
After the injury,
After the death.
Its assurance is a spectre
A ghostly layer atop our doubts, our inertia,
Our need for maps.
Look differently, too, at the cold snow,

Another ghostly layer.
Offering no solace,
Sitting atop the future.
A blank adventure.
Under it lie our prescriptions, our thin
    certainties
They pull us along,
However haltingly,
However contorted the path,
Toward the sound.

Or perhaps not.
Perhaps our verities
Lead us away, not toward.

Or perhaps the snow is a serendipity
Perhaps it frees us
But what if that freedom is false
A perilous freedom?

Should we wait
For the sun to warm us
And for the snow to melt?
Will our insurance pay anyway?

Yes, we could think on this
Until the death of the universe
Or until the sound stops.
Let's look at this a different way.
Let's walk on the new snow
At least it's exercise.

2022
Revised 2023

BLACKBIRDS

For Wallace Stevens

I

MORE than thirteen times
I've seen blackbirds,
   Birds of color that are blackbirds
And black birds
That are not blackbirds.

II

An Oriole called,
Simulating a Robin.
It was not intentional confusion.

III

A Grackle with blue head
Consorted with a Cowbird
Near some Starlings.

IV

Women I know
Have not been besieged of late
By blackbirds at their feet.

V

We strain, looking in the distance
As far as we can,
Not a blackbird in sight.
It seems a portent.

VI

In the twilight
The sudden calls of unseen blackbirds
Startle us out of our reverie.

VII

Blackbirds with red and yellow epaulets
Scold us and each other
Among the marsh reeds.
The reeds flex under them.

VIII

The Crows watch us as we watch them,
Speaking loudly of what they see.
If we could understand
I think we'd hear disdain
Inside their fear.

IX

Blackbirds walk. We walk.
Blackbirds fly into dimensions

We cannot know
And know things we cannot understand.

X

I climbed a tree
To be closer to a Blackbird.
It flew beyond me.

XI

A Vulture circled overhead,
Waiting, black as the blackest Blackbird.

XII

My rhythm
And the Blackbird's rhythm
Are not the same
Unless we agree
To be in the same space.

XIII

In this climate
The Blackbirds seldom stay
To see the snow.
A Cardinal sits loudly on the whitened branch.

June 2022

Rain Refraction

Colors as I learned them –
Sharp, clear colors,
The bright, unmuted greens
Dulled by dryness
The shock of so many browns
In a bark mulch
Newly wet
All distinct.
A rock, dappled, by the shore
Once home and dry
Is just another rock.
It helps to know why the greens are greener
The browns browner
But the knowing can't explain
Why my eyes seem quicker
My skin tingles
My heart races.

Revision of a 1980s partial poem
August 2021

IMPRESSIONIST ENCOUNTER

THIS Renoir did it, this exquisite woman.
    Magritte's macabre bent coffin puzzled
    me;
The Gauguin still life piqued my glancing eye.
But the Renoir! The woman makes me dream
As she, seen from behind in reverie,
Her head a bit inclined, her perfect hair,
Her hand a light support beside her head,
Dreams too of the day she's in, of distant days.

My mind turns in silent conversation
With imagined viewers whose vision mimics
    mine
And say,
"How perfect a line her hand makes with her
    head,
  How right her poise, how we seem to intrude
  And feel invited to a private, secret moment
  How soft her beauty."

I look again, regard her darkened eye,
A red flower, a hint of red lip, see
How her clothes in black (that black!) and
    white

Her yellow hair
Melt into the flowerscape before her.

Still beguiled, I sit quietly in a sunken
    courtyard
And emerge from the enchantment
Seeing a waterfall, a massive Henry Moore
A Maillol bronze, a Rodin, a Lipton,
All most tastefully deployed.
A man reclines before a supine nude
In parody of her and asks a friend
To snap a photo, make perpetual
His own moment of epiphany.

Becalmed, I turn yet again
And climb the steps to leave.

Revision of a 1981 poem
August 2021

A Season Postponed

Such a season this one is.
A piece of sort-of living code
   Replicates itself with joyful abandon
While we try to hide,
Hating it as if it were an intentional enemy
Trying with evil purpose to destroy joy.

Treasured times together in this season
So memorable that we recreate them every
   year:
Last-minute random wrapping, whatever's to
   hand,
Food abounding from a congeries of cooks,
Gifts obtained past the last minute,
   wonderfully whimsical,
An ocean of drink,
Cards you'd never find in a store,
The focus of the long year in a single day.
These we remember and lament
In our quiet, once again.
We want to be angry, to fight, to defeat
But the code's the code, secret and prolific
A reminder of an implacable universe

That simply is, and of the little we control,
No matter what we think, rage as we will.

The journals of our plague years will, in ages
    hence,
Surprise and amuse our distant progeny, if
    progeny there are.
Some will pity or be remotely sad
While others will parse the history
With dispassion and, perhaps,
The sense that we could have done better
Had we known what better was.

We, meanwhile, in our historical cocoon,
Unknowing as we are,
Try to find a way that our next such season
Is unconstrained;
Hoping that the dumb, frolicking code
Has grown tired or has, of its own accord,
Coded itself into oblivion.
Then we can wrap and cook and drink
Without the cast of fear that should not be
    between us.
Humans invented hope for such things.
There is, at least, that.

December 2021

UPON PASSING THE BATON

I'VE told you the story.
It was sort of an accident.
I got asked:
Would you take this job?
I was buttered up nicely:
"Your past experience."
"Your steadiness."
"You're the right person for this moment."
It didn't occur to me
That I was part of someone's plan,
A friend in court.

I took it on.
The court was an illusion,
The plan a chimera,
The motivations personal,
The results a brown field.

At the beginning we weren't in a state
That could begin to think about batons.
Far from it.
We were, instead, discovering
That the track we ran on
Had potholes and broken hurdles
And dimly drawn lanes..

Bags of bad-smelling stuff
Were thrown on the path.
But we re-drew the lanes
Filled the holes
Cleaned the track
And gathered back at the starting line.
Instead of running against one another,
We run as a team.

The trick now
Is to show those who don't see the track or
Who don't know there's a race to run together
Or who are running in place or into the past
That, when they ask, "But where would we
    go?"
We say, as a certain wizard says: "On!"

We move on because
That's what we're here to do,
Because there's joy in it
Because it's time that we did.
We move on without those
Who need to reside in their past,
Who need to tell their realities to each other,
However sad and false.

I move on because I seek different joy
Sharing my vision in a different way
Wanting to see others flourish
Wanting to stand behind them
Wanting to give them ways to clear their own
    paths
To plant the new trees
To hear different music.

Take the baton we fashioned
It's no longer my time.
It's your time.
Live it well.

April 2022

Perepeteia

Her blondish locks, once long, down to her
    waist
Now shoulder-short and matchéd to her skin;
Mine lost to time, replaced by polished dome,
And both of us more careful in our pace.
Our years together nearing fifty-eight
Yet still we carry on without surcease,
Perfervid more than less in our belief
That much remains ahead for us to do.
However much we know each of the other,
We're still surprised, though more amused
    than shocked,
At learning yet another thing or two
About a past event or inward thought.
Thus do we live into an aging grace
Each morning seeing each a lovéd face.

April 2021

WHAT I MIGHT HAVE DONE

IF I could do it all over . . .
An impossible idea
Seeming to be full of regret,
To reek of remorse,
Promising to sink a person into a certain
    melancholy.

Yet assessment points occur
If we live long enough.
I've found myself there several times,
Times that have sprinkled my mind with
"What if?" and "Well, maybe."
But now that I'm thinking on it I understand
That a kind of joy can spark "Could have
    been."
Not "Might have been." Or "Should have
    been."

Were there reason to do it
I'd have retained the French
That my mother spoke to me in my first 3
    years.
Oh, I learned a lot more of it in school, yes.

And I retrieved it in France in a surprising
    way once.
The piano I didn't have made the lessons I
    took strange.
Had I had a piano
It was clear that I would have been decent at
    it,
Able to plink, at least, without hesitation.
And I'd have learned far more about music
Than I know today in the splotches of
    impression
That I can display at will.

The teaching I did, even trained for
Was so exhilarating at times -
That class that fully connected
With each other, with me,
The woman who could not write,
Then could: a bright moment for her,
For them
For me.

But life intruded, as it always does
Life demanded a different path

It was temporary.
Then it wasn't.

And here I sit, remembering,
Not regretting; just vividly remembering,
Rehearsing, with a private grin
Things I could have done,
Or so I think.

October 2022

EARLIER POEMS

Adelaide Crapsey (1878 – 1914)

From The Poetry Foundation

https://www.poetryfoundation.org/poets/adelai
de-crapsey

"[An] important component in Crapsey's work was her reliance on the methods of Japanese tanka and haiku. With her invention of the cinquain, Crapsey created an American form similar to these Japanese predecessors. Like Ezra Pound, she admired the Japanese poets for their compressed language and formal aesthetics. The five unrhymed lines of the cinquain followed strict accentual-syllabic requirements. The lines consisted of two, four, six, eight, and two syllables (or accents), respectively. In addition to her preferred metrical scheme . . . Crapsey strove for a kind superposition of ideas similar to the "break," or sudden perception of truth typically found in Japanese haiku."

CINQUAINS

After Adelaide Crapsey

AUGUST

SOME sun,
Already hot
With just a pizza slice
Burning the eastern sky at dawn,
Fries dreams.

LATE MARCH

Sparrow
Piping into
A gray day's early light;
Crocus, yellow-green in dank mist;
Brown grass.

(WE) PRAISE (US)

Mozart
Alleluia
Joy shouts across the years
Exultation, jubilation
Rorem

Echidnas and Platypuses

It's not
That monotremes
(Literally "one-holes")
Either don't dream or have duck bills
That's strange.

Alarm

What time
Have we to find
The faith in self enough
To give the world the hope it needs?
What time?

1987

Sunday

JORDAN

Bursts by
One man, into
Three, Baryshnikov flight
Leans in, arm swirling, shifts hands, flips
Netless.

PRAIRIE CONVERSATIONS

Summer:
Corn tassel waves.
Winter: roofs in long rows,
Wind-whipped wood smoke, white black
    white roads.
Spring: lawns.

1987

PLAIN SENSE

GROWING up among hills
I learned to think hill thoughts,
Learned the art of darting
From one to another thing.
You, who live in this flat land,
Cannot have that sort of thinking
Or that haste.
Staring across those miles
Your world's abrupt surprises
Come sneaking up behind you
In your moments of transfixion.
Electrical storms (always a shock to us,
Leaping over hilltops)
Here build on a long horizon,
Ominous moving walls,
But they don't boil up unannounced.
Your meditations inside the long gaze
Need not be interrupted.
You draw sustenance from the chaos
Displaying on the wide screen before you.
You do not need our fever, our quick-eyed,
    clipped accents

To be in these precincts.
Forgive my thinking you slow-witted.
My thoughts showed: that may be why
You brought me out into this landscape
Planting us here to feel
The long pulse of the earth.

2023

OTHER CINQUAINS

THIS odd November morning,
    Reprise of spring
(The time is wrong for harbingers),
I sit out, looking deep
Into brown woods
So recently secret
Steamy, buzzing.

This quiet day
With crickets, calling birds, warm haziness . . .
So still
That from the half-bare oak tree
I hear a simple leaf
Ticking through the others
As it feathers down.

A sudden breeze
Darts noiseless out of the woods,
Slices
To that primitive locus
In my soul
Which knows the face of winter
And hunkers down before it.

The fuzzy warmth of a moment ago
Returns but cannot restore
My half-eyed languor;
A solitary warbler, abruptly silent
Moves hastily from tree to tree.

1983

OFF THE MAIN LINE

THIS abandoned track goes rusty into the
woods.
I followed it once for miles but
Didn't find its end
Or any hint of it.
It might have been a high-speed line, I think,
Running through gentle curves,
Cutting noisy through the culverts.
A tree grows in the roadbed here,
Matter-of-factly lifting ties and rails
With persistent, silent roots.
A sudden ramp and platform
Stand lichened and mossed, alone
In the copse below the hill.
A curling, leaning fence comes
Crazily out of the woods and crosses the track
In the clearing ahead. I hesitate, entranced:
What kind of place was it
That someone hurried to along this track?
All that seems left of it
Is the way to get there,
Blocked as it is by the lurching fence.

I don't go further -

Not afraid, you understand;
It's just . . . a place that tried
So hard to keep the past out
Doesn't want the present in it, does it?
From a wrinkle in the landscape
This road to someone's old and hidden
    somewhere
Appears and disappears across a meadow,
Winds in twin brown ribbons up a hill
And faces into the hazy afternoon.

1980

THE CAPE HIGHWAY

December 28, 1979

PURPLE red-edged clouds
　　Laid long against the horizon . . .

Vast island nations

Looming out of a blood-blue sea . . .

Perspectives shifting . . .

We came over the hill

To the dying arc of the evening sun

You in the front seat

In the small private world of your conversation

I alone in back

Finishing the whistled coda of a trumpet
　　voluntary

Unintended herald

To the alien world I found

As we crested the hill

Heading west.

1980

RELATIONS

THIS book
Erased the world around me,
Plunged without obstruction
To my well-defined center;
It consumed my mind and being.

I send it to you because
You did the same
To equal depths.
I thought
You and the book might be related
And could speak, each to the other.

I have written nothing in the book
About any of this.

1982

VESPER SILHOUETTE

THEY embrace before the window.
The graceful curving line
Of body meeting body,
Crimsoned by the setting sun,
Deepens, darkens red to black
As they turn their stately turn,
Their cardinal contredanse
To the rhythm of a slow and private music.

1980

SHAMAN OF SPRING

I

I am Shaman of Spring
Priest and doctor to
The pagan mysteries beneath the snow:
I bid them grow and flower.
In cold, enduring Winter they
Follow their own subglacial urgings
Beyond my best and strongest incantations:
Their ken is not of me.
Canny then, crafty, I become
Smug repository for the nonce,
Wait out persistent Winter,
Burn logs against recurring darks.
With magic I ward off the chill
That creeps through the imagination

I wait and hear the shuffle of transformation
And the soul's pedalpoint throbs uncertainly
Lacking the harmonies of warmer climates

II

I am
A slow and slower walker

In frozen lands descending
All fuel
Burned to ash.

I recognize this landscape without feature;
I've been and lived for trackless eons here
Humming monotonic threnodies
Thrums
Against the loss of ancient voices,
Witless, hearing dim, fading sounds
Beneath the ice.

III

A simple act: a touch,
A poet's touch of fire to frozen music
Making live a silent, barren magic.
An olden, parchéd throat
Long out of practice
Begins a croaking song.

IV

Voice and ear contrive to build
A chord to pierce this most unwilling tundra,
To find the fundamental
That rings with the secret things

Faintly calling through the permafrost.
Once found, this chant rolls to raucous song,
And a circling, mad dance bursts forth,
A green and limber chorus rising out
Into the sun.

V

I am Shaman of Spring
Crier of all new-found verdancy,
Minstrel of the cycles and
Change-ringer for the celebration.

1980

AT THE CLINIC

DOORS open everywhere and names are called
"BridgetCarlaNancy" down one hall
Orthopedic cases crutching by
A screaming kid with something in his eye
"Lily? Where is Lily? Are you here?
The doctor's waiting, Lily!" Now, that's queer
Did Lily leave? Did she not want to stay
For good news? Bad news? Hope another day
Would make it better? People slide behind
The door. This is a ritual designed
As living trompe l'oeil. They seem to look
The same when they come out as when they took
The call to go in. Pregnant ladies limping
Ladies. Men with walkers. Young girls primping
Reading pamphlets on maternal good
Nutrition. I am watching. Eyelids hood
The vision darkens I'm asleep I start
Awake a large old woman struggles farts

To get out of her chair. My daughter's there
She says it's time to leave. Was I aware
That I had snored? Two people smile at me
As we walk off to pay the massive fee.

1987

LIFE

THE spot on the road slowly
 Grows to a lump. Fascinated, as always,
I already aim away from it
As always.
till too far away to know
Exactly what this downed thing is;
I tighten when some change in light tells me
It is still moving.
I silently speak to the cars around me
Telling them to have a care
To go around it
To miss.
The distance narrows. I see now
How agitatedly it moves,
How its helplessness
Is like my own.
A car seems to straddle it. My belly leaps.
The lump still moves; I close on it.
Its pages cease their flailing in the wind

All animation gone.
The ritual ends.
As usual.
I pass.
Another thing lies flattened in the road.

1985

Continued

IT'S a leaf, he said,
A member of the maples,
Indigenous to northern climes.
Falls every year, comes back
Without fail.
It fell, she said,
To let the world take on a new look,
To be the last perfect touch
To autumn's pattern;
To experience its full potential.
Yes, he said, clever.
It's a rock, he said,
A major metamorphic
Used at one time to make weapons,
Shaped by the wind, water
Or the hunter.
It signifies, she said,
The struggle of nature against itself:
Pound or be pounded by
The other forces,
An eternal fight for existence.
Yes, he said, forever.

It's a Miracle, she said,
That you find constancy
In falling leaves, purpose in rocks.
I have so much to see
Through your eyes.
I fear, he said,
That you are not the leaf or the rock.
You are the wind blowing free
Scattering leaves and shaping rocks
Then disappearing.
No, she said, never.

1980s

Chairs

I

In a friend's gallery
Years back, in another life
I viewed a chair.
It was in a darkened room.
It stood on four uneven legs
And was illuminated by one small spotlight
Placed high above it off to the side.
It cast somber shadows.
This piece's name was a part of the display:
"Dejection" or "Alone" or "Lost Aspirations" -
Something in that line.
I told the gallerist that the light
Was misplaced. She never did
Forgive me.

II

An alembic is an apparatus for distilling.
More to the point:
It is a thing that purifies or transforms
By a process like distilling.
Now, it isn't fair to judge art

From half-tones in the newspaper.
Today I saw a photograph of a construction
Having the name "Alembic". It is,
Apparently,
The second in a series.
It looks like a free-standing
Chair leg
With two rungs angling from its top
And a railing around its rungs.
It also looks like a
Right-angled highway with a guard rail
At the scenic overlook.
I suppose it is a distillation.
What is purified is in question.

1989

FLIGHT 83

THE angles and planes of your beautiful face
A slow collapse as you drink talk.
Pouring your wine in life out to this man.
You talk of hurts and things as they should be.
His whiskey-colored glasses hide his eyes,
This man with grey and yellow hair and all
The places of his life in fine routelines
Etched in red along his cheeks and nose.
You open your life's faucet to this man
Who gives you all the reassuring words;
Who, as the roads below get larger now
Leans into you and whispers. I can't hear.
And did those things become as they should
    be?
And what's his name: is he still listening?

1987

DREAM IN G

A green day with music,
Its heat oppressive as I ascend into it
Its harmonies
Subtle, soft with sweat.
I half-wake to a vision dream,
To long drifting wisps
Of times real and imagined,
Times that were yours.
An ancient air play
Plaintive and soaring
Paean to my mood. I dream
Of Donne and speak to the sun
Busie olde foole that it is.
I dream
Of lying here
To this music
In this heat
Saying to your hair
"Shall we find some Brueghel? Some Matisse?

Wander down tree-lined streets
Lazily, laughing, looking in windows?
Shall we parcel out and brew
Small quantities of coffee in cafés
And talk of Lear and Falstaff?"
Idle thoughts slow motion waking
Vaporizing dream of love words
As they softly echo echo echo
Into silence.

1982

EUBIE

(To Eubie Blake, Ragtime Guy)

LONG fingers laid flat to the keys
(They say you could span 15 to the hand)
You played across a century.
When we found the long silent music of our
    history
There you were, waiting,
The joyful survivor of obscurity
Ready to play.
Joplin, dead 50 years,
Was pulled from the dust and daguerreotypes
A sad, lordly figure,
A ghost on a piano roll,
His delicate constructions
Come alive again, no hint of the cathouse.
No, no hint. Joplin gave us
The ethereal, the careful, the emotional.
Jelly Roll gave us blowsy, loud
Whorehouse anthems,
Tigers roaring in rut.
But it took historians and preservers
To bring them to us.

You were the only ambassador
From that ragged time.
Nimble, laughing,
You made us look and remember,
Look and listen and dance.
You lived a century.
And after you were sure we'd noticed,
You smiled, thought a tune
And died.

1983

ABOUT THE AUTHOR

ED MCDEVITT was born and brought up near Boston. He carried on a varied career, the last half of which resided in information technology. He is an architecture and public art docent in Chicago, near which he has lived for 40 years. He discovered years ago that Chicago has one of the world's largest collections of public art and tried to document all of it, proving that assessing the scope of an endeavor is not one of his strengths.

He is a capable if unremarkable high tenor in a fine church choir and has a life-long abiding interest in things musical. He has a strange tendency to become the head of volunteer organizations that he is a part of and to swear never to do it again.

One of his odd talents is that he's a very fast touch typist, which is why, when he's not head of an organization, he's its recording secretary.

He will soon celebrate his 60th anniversary with his wife, Judith and will garnish the celebration with his two adult children and their very significant others.

He writes an occasional blog on many topics, is an inveterate letter-to-the-editor creator, and is an unapologetic liberal thinker.

None of this sheds light on why he also writes poetry. It's a conundrum and we'll leave it at that.

www.ingramcontent.com/pod-product-compliance
Lightning Source LLC
Chambersburg PA
CBHW020642160726
47991CB00003B/981